D0046842

THE NEW NORMAL

THE
new
NORMAL

LifeChange Books

JILL BRISCOE

Multnomah® Publishers *Sisters, Oregon*

THE NEW NORMAL
published by Multnomah Publishers, Inc.
Published in association with the literary agency of Alive Communications, Inc.
7680 Goddard Street, Suite 200, Colorado Springs, CO 80920

© 2005 by Jill Briscoe
International Standard Book Number: 1-59052-473-X

Cover design by Kirk DouPonce, DogEaredDesign.com
Cover image by Martin Barraud/Getty Images

Unless otherwise indicated, Scripture quotations are from:
The Holy Bible, New International Version © 1973, 1984 by International Bible Society,
used by permission of Zondervan Publishing House
Other Scripture quotations are from:
New American Standard Bible® (NASB) © 1960, 1977, 1995
by the Lockman Foundation. Used by permission.
The Holy Bible, New King James Version (NKJV) © 1984 by Thomas Nelson, Inc.
The Holy Bible, King James Version (KJV)
Holy Bible, New Living Translation (NLT) © 1996. Used by permission of Tyndale House
Publishers, Inc. All rights reserved.
The Message © 1993, 1994, 1995, 1996, 2000, 2001, 2002
Used by permission of NavPress Publishing Group
Contemporary English Version (CEV) © 1995 by American Bible Society
The Holy Bible, *English Standard Version* (ESV) © 2001 by Crossway Bibles, a division of Good
News Publishers. Used by permission. All rights reserved.
The New English Bible (NEB) © 1961, 1970 by the Delegates of the Oxford University Press and
the Syndics of the Cambridge University Press

Multnomah is a trademark of Multnomah Publishers, Inc., and is registered in the U.S. Patent and
Trademark Office. The colophon is a trademark of Multnomah Publishers, Inc.

Printed in the United States of America

ALL RIGHTS RESERVED
No part of this publication may be reproduced, stored in a retrieval system,
or transmitted, in any form or by any means—electronic, mechanical, photocopying,
recording, or otherwise—without prior written permission.

For information:
MULTNOMAH PUBLISHERS, INC. • 601 NORTH LARCH ST. • SISTERS, OR 97759

Library of Congress Cataloging-in-Publication Data

Briscoe, Jill.
  The new normal / Jill Briscoe.
    p. cm.
  ISBN 1-59052-473-X
  1. Christian life. 2. Trust in God. 3. Briscoe, Jill. I. Title.
BV4501.3.B754 2005
248.4—dc22

                                              2005018509

05 06 07 08 09 10—10 9 8 7 6 5 4 3 2 1 0

CONTENTS

BELIEVING WHAT
YOU BELIEVE

There is nothing like a crisis to really focus the mind on the things that matter. Flying back from Russia to the States on September 11, 2001, I was caught high above the Atlantic when the planes hit their targets. And we, the world, entered the *new normal*. In that moment, I had every reason to revisit my faith in a hurry and decide whether I believed what I believed! Was God on my plane? Did He fly United? Or was He attending to some universal business in another sphere? Did He miss the incident altogether and have to wait to see it on network news?

At times like this we know we should have faith that

God is on His throne, thoroughly cognizant and in charge, undisputed King of the universe. But if we are honest, at times like this we struggle with our faith.

Where was God on September 11, when the planes struck the twin towers and the Pentagon, and nose-dived into a field in Pennsylvania? Since that momentous event, and despite new and horrible cover stories of atrocities all over the world, people all are still asking that question. *Where was God that day?* The world was stunned by the terrorism that changed our lives forever. Christians found their faith put to the test. I was no exception.

Christians are supposed to believe that they know what God is about—in general, that is! When a 9/11 happens, we're thrown off. I thought I believed in God's power and ever-present presence with all my heart! But did I still believe it that terrible day, when the sun stopped shining and everyone was told to get out the emergency card (the one no one bothers reading on "ordinary" flights!) from the seat pocket in front of them?

In former times, when crisis hit, I was able to fix my heart on what I know about God. As a child, I lived through the Second World War, and as an adult I weathered the doctor's death sentence when my father and mother were diagnosed with terminal cancer. I also struggled through difficult adjustments as we left our homeland and emigrated to another culture, where we raised our children. I suppose I have had my share of critical moments that one would experience when he or she lives in a fallen world among fallen people with a fallen nature.

But the Bible has led me to believe that though I may be out of control, God isn't. He hasn't abdicated, isn't on vacation, and hasn't left town. He hasn't abandoned the universe. He hasn't lost His touch and isn't traumatized by any events on earth. He isn't in therapy and hasn't retired. He's alive and well, and He reigns supreme, indisputable King of kings and Lord of lords.

As the book of Revelation tells us, He is the first and the last and everything else in between. "'I am the Alpha and the Omega,' says the Lord God, 'who is, and who was, and who is to come, the Almighty'" (Revelation 1:8). I had done moderately well with this in the past—especially where flying was concerned—but this 9/11 trauma was a new test for me.

I revisited the days in my mind when I found it well-nigh impossible to get myself on a plane at all. I had flown little when we immigrated to America in 1970. I would try not to look out of the window and would select a seat toward the front of the plane by an emergency exit. One day, I had to travel to Los Angeles from Wisconsin. (I was to speak at an important gathering on the subject of faith, if you can believe it!) Sitting in my seat, my heart pounding, I reviewed my notes. I couldn't concentrate, as it was a windy day and a rough flight. *How can I dare get off this plane and talk about trusting God?* I asked myself.

I was to discover a peace that wouldn't quit and that flooded my heart and soul and left me gasping with grace.

Sitting there miserably, I shut my eyes and asked the Lord to give me some word of comfort. Nothing came. *Okay,* I thought, *then what word of comfort from the Scriptures has He given me already?* Sometimes we look to God for some new word or experience when all the time "the word is near"—even in our hearts (Romans 10:8; Deuteronomy 30:14). A well-known and loved Scripture came to mind in that moment as if it had been waiting patiently for its cue to walk onto the stage of my life. "Without faith it is impossible to please God, because anyone who comes to him must believe that he exists and that he rewards those who earnestly seek him

(Hebrews 11:6). What would be the reward of my earnest heart's cry? I was to discover a peace that wouldn't quit and that flooded my heart and soul and left me gasping with grace. I settled back into my seat as Grace graced me, and I knew that this battle was over (till the next time).

On September 11, God reminded me of that particular truth I had laid up in my heart years before. Like a squirrel in winter, I unearthed the fruit of knowledge laid away for such a time as this, and it nourished my soul. The pilot came on the intercom and told us there was a national emergency and that all the airspace and borders of the United States were closed—but he couldn't tell us why until he got the plane down in Newfoundland. And I sat my soul down and asked sternly, "What do you believe about what you believe, Jill? Has the character of God suddenly changed? Is Jesus Christ the same yesterday, today, and forever? Do I really believe that 'God is'?" My soul assured me firmly that I really *did* believe that He doesn't change.

Whatever shakes my world cannot shake His. He cannot be shaken. He is never caught off guard. He cannot be moved. He has not suddenly become subnormal or abnormal. He wasn't either the old normal or the new normal that terrible day when death intruded into our happy little world and reminded us that life is brief, a mere wisp of a thing, a passing sigh. God's supernormal reality remains intact, even when everything else is falling apart. He's then, now, and always supernormal. He was who He was, and is who He is, and will be who He will be. He promised. And "God is not a man, that he should lie" (Numbers 23:19). What's more, as Job acknowledged, "I know that you can do all things; no plan of yours can be thwarted" (Job 42:1–2).

Some of you have no argument with all of this, except perhaps to wrestle with the idea that God's plan could permit a 9/11 to happen when He had the power to stop it. You have said to me, "Jill, I believe He is who He says He is. Unbelief isn't my problem. It's not 'who' He is, but 'where' He is, or rather where He 'was' or 'wasn't' on 9/11 or some other dark, terrible day of my life that bothers me. Was He sleeping on the job?" C. S. Lewis says: "We talk of him loudly as if He is present, but secretly we think of him as being absent." In my head I thought of Him as being present on September 11, but in my heart I wasn't so sure I could put it all together.

Secretly (for we pride ourselves on being card-carrying Christians who would never have a question like this) some of us are tempted to think He went AWOL. And that would be understandable—He's very busy! Well, *that* doesn't sound right either, does it? In the end, it depends on whether your beliefs affect your reaction to the unpleasant surprises that life throws at you—or whether He can calm your beating heart and hush your fears to sleep.

WHY DOESN'T HE DO SOMETHING?

The problem with 9/11 experiences is that we are tempted to believe that if we do not see Him take action, He mustn't have been there at all. After all, if He had been, He surely would have intervened—like Superman. Why didn't He swoop out of the skies and catch those planes before they hit their targets? Why didn't He stop it from happening? This is our true dilemma. How can we believe He was there—and sat on His hands?

But the thing is, He isn't Superman—He is Super God! So much the better!

Today in America military families are asking these same questions. Why didn't He stop the grenade in Afghanistan or defuse the fatal bomb in Iraq? Our church asked the agonizing question, "Was He asleep on the day two of our missionaries were walking to work in

Uganda and wicked men came out of the jungle and murdered them?" What about the tsunami in Asia? An act of God, so they say.

Or coming nearer to home, what about the twelve-year-old who got lost in the mountains, never to be found, or the child raped and killed in my home state? Wasn't He there? Didn't He care?

Why, oh why, didn't He *do* something?

Chapter One

YOUR OWN
GROUND ZERO

Some of you have experienced your own ground zero since 2001.

Trauma comes calling at will. Or so it seems. For many of us it wasn't September 11 but August 15 or July 1 or some other date that is etched in our memory. We have not been traumatized so much by the carnage in New York City but by a different disaster.

Perhaps it came upon us out of a clear blue sky, just like the two planes over Manhattan. Maybe we got up one morning, and it seemed like any other day in our lives. But then without warning, death came. Maybe it was the death of a marriage. We may have come home to the proverbial note on the table telling us a spouse has gone. Or maybe a knock on the door ushered you into the nightmare of a son or daughter in trouble with the police. Where is God when the crisis hits and we are left with our faith, gasping for breath? Today these questions have become part of the air we breathe—part of lives lived out in the new normal.

I have friends who very recently have experienced the death of a relationship, the passing of a parent or a friend. Others close to me have suffered the demise of a career or a dream they had for a child, a dream that has turned into a nightmare.

These things happen, and the ground shakes. Our world collapses. Some of us have had the twin towers of our self-esteem and our God-esteem destroyed in *one day,* and our faith is reeling. We should have seen the planes heading our way, we chide ourselves. Maybe we could have alerted others to the danger and reduced the numbers of casualties.

Perhaps one of our married children has told us that she is getting an abortion. We were hoping to be first-time grandparents, and now there will be no baby to celebrate. Maybe the emotional pain is so great that you feel *you* have had an abortion, too. Maybe a husband has been unfaithful. Perhaps in addition to the betrayal, it resulted in disease—even AIDS.

Now that's a 9/11.

These things have all happened since the planes flew into the towers (they happened before 9/11, too), so now we don't just have the chronic "old normal" fear we are used to that pervades our waking moments. We are experiencing a "new normal" fear, too. A feeling of dread and acute discomfort layered on top of the old normal feeling of dread and discomfort, as we wait for the other shoe to drop.

Many of us are trying our best to adjust to the new normal paradigm. But we are told by experts in our society that there is more anxiety, depression, panic, and pessimism across all classes, creeds, and ages, and nothing seems to help. Welcome to a new day lived in this state of mind, this present distress, this underlying uneasiness—a sense of "Things are not the way they ought to be."

THE FRUSTRATION FACTOR

So how *are* we coping with it all? We all react differently to frustration with things we can't control. Do we find ourselves stamping our spiritual feet in a faith tantrum and throwing our toys out of the crib? Do we demand our old normal back again so we can settle down to being our thoroughly selfish selves? Do we hate the new normal? Do we pout and sulk? Have we decided to punish God by not talking to Him? That does no good, of course. Such silliness simply cuts us off from our only source of help! The present crisis is still the present crisis. We are still held hostage to fear, apprehension, frustration, depression, and often despair.

Do we hate the new normal? Do we pout and sulk? Have we decided to punish God by not talking to Him?

After returning home from my foray into Newfoundland and an interesting six and a half days in a Salvation Army hall sleeping on a cot, I noticed that I wasn't sleeping well. Instead of counting sheep, I was counting terrorists. I looked around and saw my friends dealing with the new normal in other different ways. We heard pundits saying, "Things will never be the same again." And we wanted to prove them wrong, especially Christians. Some of us turned to food for comfort. Yet even globs of ice cream and tons of French fries failed to bring us peace of mind We tried shopping (a friend calls it retail therapy) to no avail. Accumulation led to more frustration, as more is never enough!

TV seems like a good distraction. During those first days following the crash of the towers in 2001, *Sex and the City* was one of the most-watched shows in America. We were apparently longing for the comfort of intimacy, yet living in our new normal seemed only to accelerate the broken relationships that lay scattered all over the landscape. At the end of one episode of *Sex and the City,* an actress commented that even after many relationships, her heart was "still a lonely hunter."

How sad! Even the most intimate relationships are not where real inner peace and comfort are found. No man can ever love you enough, no child can ever need you enough, no friend can ever console you enough— only Jesus can do all that and bring peace! God is the God of all comfort (2 Corinthians 1:3), and we must turn to Him to deal with the frustration factor in our lives. Yet so many in the world today are searching for peace and comfort in just this way.

There have, after all, been new normal traumas since Adam was a lad! Way back when, in the first century, the apostle Paul talked about a very real and present crisis (1 Corinthian 7:26) that had disrupted everyone's life as much as the terrorists disrupted ours. It was certainly affecting the most personal relationships in families and in the church. That's what a good crisis does.

THE FEAR FACTOR

I love that you can find parallel circumstances in the Bible that mirror what is going on today. The culture and the time may be different, but a crisis is a crisis. And we all understand what it's like regardless of the date.

In the first century, when Paul was writing to new believers about how the old ways of doing things didn't pertain anymore, he was facing a threefold crisis: in the church, in Corinth, and in his world. In his letter, he told immature believers in a pagan culture in a world gone mad: "Because of the present crisis, I think that it is good for you to remain as you are" (1 Corinthians 7:26). That is, "If you're married, stay married. If you aren't, put your plans on hold."

Relationships were in turmoil because of their particular crisis, just as relationships are in turmoil now. There was major anxiety everywhere, particularly within families. People were worried about their loved ones. What would happen to them? In verse 32 (NLT), Paul advised, "In everything you do, I want you to be free from the concerns of this life" (as it pertained, among other things, to relationships). He was worried about them being worried. "I want you to be free from anxious care," he says (NEB). In this our new normal, we can all relate to this. We too are thinking about homeland security and our family's safety, aren't we?

In my position as minister-at-large for my home church, I travel a lot. Immediately after 9/11, I had the extraordinary experience of feeling safer outside the country than within. And now that things have calmed down a little in the U.S., they have heated up abroad! No one is feeling secure anywhere anymore, or so it seems.

This is the new normal.

Yet the new normal is just the old normal in your face! Nothing has really changed. Evil is evil. Right is right. Men's hearts were failing them for fear well before the events of the eleventh, just as they were before the events in Paul's day. Yet God is still on His throne. So the new normal is only life after the Fall, lived in a fallen environment with a sinful nature—but then so was the old normal. It's just that sin seems to abound more obviously and flagrantly now. But God *is* still on His throne.

We have such a short amount of time, Paul argues, to do the Lord's work. The real problem facing the

Corinthians (and us) was the proper expenditure of time and energy. Paul wants us to devote our time and abilities to works of service and devotion to God, which we can do better if we are unmarried (vv. 32, 34).

Frustration can morph into fear. Paul addresses this fear factor. The frustration that results when we can't have the world our way can morph into fear as we realize that we are out of control. Fear was certainly dominating the new believers' lives when Paul wrote his letter to the Corinthians. And the apostle wanted them free from inordinate, obsessive, paralyzing fear.

What was behind this fear in the church in Corinth? Apparently there was a real attack on their security—a very real and present danger of some sort. It could have been persecution. Paul wanted to spare Christians from seeing their loved ones tortured or expelled from their homes. We are often tempted to believe that *our* crisis is the worst that has ever happened to anyone, but the crisis for the Corinthians was as brutal as any. The emperor Claudius ruled Paul's world AD 41–54. Fortunately, his wife did a service to the world by poisoning him. But then she brought up Nero, Claudius's adopted son, to be another nasty, Christian-hating emperor.

Paul's letter to the Corinthians arrived while

Claudius was still alive and ruling. Many of them fled to Corinth and other towns in the empire while Paul was busy establishing the church in these places. The emperor expelled Jews from Rome for rioting and punished what he called tomb robbers and Jewish agitators. A prophet named Agabus predicted a famine, which happened during Claudius's reign. This caused great hardship in the empire.

The "present crisis" Paul talked about could have been all of the above or a crisis in Corinth itself as a new Christian culture clashed with a pagan culture in sin city (as it was known in the ancient world).

"It isn't who is in any great White House that matters in the end; it is who is on the Great White Throne!"

Whatever the Corinthian crisis was, Paul picked up his pen and wrote to the new believers in Corinth, pointing out that regardless of who was ruling the country, God was ruling the *world*. Paul wanted the Corinthians (and us) to rest in that fact. My husband has reminded our congregation from the pulpit: "It isn't who is in any great White House that matters in the end; it is who is on the Great White Throne!" Do we concur? We Jesus lovers and glory givers who seek to honor God must not allow the fear factor to cause us heart failure.

It seems to me that the world is experiencing a massive heart attack. Our hearts are failing us for fear. Shortly after 9/11, Osama bin Laden was reported to say, "From north to south, from east to west, Americans are living in fear. For this we thank God." Every so often, the man surfaces and beats the fear drum on videotape.

Before this happened, Americans had tended to believe *anywhere but here*. Acts of terrorism, massive casualties, and tragedies happen outside our shores, but not *here*. Anywhere except America. Yet someone at the time commented: "Exceptionalism has been blown away in shards." I think that's true. But we shouldn't be surprised. Didn't Jesus say: "In this world you *will* have trouble" (John 16:33)? He didn't say, "In the world you *may or may not* have trouble," or, "It would be nice if you didn't have any trouble," or, "I'm not sure how much trouble you'll have," or, "I'll save you from every little bit of trouble that comes your way," but rather, "In the world you *will* have trouble"! So the fear factor must be faced and dealt with by the *faith factor*. And the faith factor is rooted in the Father factor.

THE FATHER FACTOR

The Father factor is so important. It isn't how much faith we have; it's a matter of in Whom or What we place that faith. If we have faith in someone or something that is untrustworthy, then our faith will do us no good at all. But if we put our faith in someone or something that is reliable and worthy of our faith, the results will be very different.

My husband, Stuart, gives a good illustration of this. He talks about putting your faith in very thick ice covering a body of water and staying safe and dry. However, if you put all your weight onto thin ice, you could drown by faith! You see, it's not the amount of your faith that's the most important thing; it's what you put your faith in. When you have faith in the heavenly Father, you will not drown! This is the Father factor.

THE FAITH FACTOR

If you happen to be right in the middle of a crisis at the moment, or if one looms dark on the horizon, ask yourself, "Is the Father omnipresent or is He omniabsent?" When you find yourself standing at your own personal ground zero, affirm out loud, "I believe in *God*!" whether you see evidence of His immediate presence or not.

Matthew Henry said: "The God of Israel, the Savior, is sometimes a God who hides himself, but never a God who absents himself. Sometimes in the dark, but never at a distance." *He never absents Himself.*

"Well, He sure could have fooled me," you mutter under your evangelical breath. But that skepticism is because you presume that if He *were* present, He would have intervened in your situation or forced people to behave differently.

But God does not make people behave as they should. He gives us that most frightening and precious gift of free will. We can choose to believe or not to believe. Did Jesus make the soldiers who were killing Him believe in Him? No. No more did He make them behave as they should. Remember, God was in Christ, reconciling the world to Himself. Did Jesus force Pilate to set Him free? No.

The Jews insisted, "We have a law, and accord-ing to that law he must die, because he claimed to be the Son of God." When Pilate heard this, he was even more afraid, and he went back inside the palace. "Where do you come from," he asked Jesus, but Jesus gave him no answer.

"Do you refuse to speak to me?" Pilate said. "Don't you realize I have power either to free you or to crucify you?" Jesus answered, "You would have no power over me if it were not given to you from above."

Being present does not mean He will violate the most sacred freedom He ordained for every son of Adam and daughter of Eve: the freedom to choose our actions and behaviors. Pilate had been given the freedom to choose what to do with Christ. "You would have no power over me if it were not given to you from above," Jesus said (v. 11). So Pilate chose to wash His hands of Jesus. Quite impossible, of course—a vote to stay neutral is a vote *against* God.

Think about it. Every human being is given the choice to wash his or her hands of the tiresome rules and regulations that govern human behavior as God ordained it. Or we can submit to His rules for life: goodness, integrity, and moral rectitude as revealed in the Word of God.

Could God have intervened on September 11? Yes. Did He? No.

Could He have intervened in your court case and forced your adversary to tell the truth instead of presenting a pack of lies? Yes. Did He? No.

What about reversing the fatal disease your father had? Could He have saved you from losing your job, your home, your child? Yes. Did He? No.

For these reasons, many have not a crisis of fear, but rather a crisis of *faith*. And before we truly have faith in Him again, we want an explanation as to why—when He could have done something, said something, changed someone—He didn't! In the end, much of it is a mystery.

My fellow passengers on United flight 929 had many questions in the days following our forced stay in Gambo, Newfoundland. I found myself trying to answer their queries concerning God's behavior. "We minuscule humans can't hold God responsible and accountable for His actions or lack thereof," I told an angry young woman. "He holds *us* accountable for our response and reaction to what, in His sovereign, mysterious will, He deems to allow."

A mystery is a secret, and God has every right to have His secrets.

In our society, that argument fails to register! Don't we have "the right to know" everything about everyone and everything everyone else knows? We may even convince ourselves that we have the right to know everything God knows. But the truth of the matter is that God has a perfect right to reveal exactly what He chooses to reveal to us—and to keep the rest a mystery.

God doesn't explain some things because our little, finite minds cannot grasp the infinite. But in grace He tells us about others things our minds *can* grasp. What a delight it was for me to tell my new friends from the plane about a verse from the Old Testament: "The secret things belong to the LORD our God, but the things revealed belong to us and to our children forever" (Deuteronomy 29:29).

Most days, one young man would debate with me for at least an hour about life in general and our crisis in particular. He would sit down with a cup of coffee and say, "Okay, Jill, what's the subject today?" And he would usually want to choose it. One day he said, "This is my question for you today. Why did God make Lucifer? If, as you say, God knew what would happen, and if He gave His angels the freedom to choose their actions, why did He make them all in the first place?"

"You know," I began, "it's a secret. It says in Deuteronomy: 'The secret things belong to the LORD our God, but the things revealed belong to us and to our children forever.'"

He looked at me.

"What you're asking me belongs to the secret things—the mysteries of God. He knows that our finite 'dust minds' can't grasp such things. There are many mysteries about life and death, and God has every right to have secrets. The reverse of what we'd like is actually true: He holds *us* accountable for *our* secrets! And He will certainly call us to account for what He has already revealed to us for our children."

We argued around the subject for a couple hours, and in the end, the young man asked "Well, okay, so just what has God revealed about the mystery of suffering in the world?"

"I'm so glad you asked me!" I replied. "Let me tell you some of the things God has said about suffering." I proceeded to tell him some truths from Scripture:

1. God made a perfect world.
2. Sin spoiled that perfect world, and sinners are now running it. So what do you expect?
3. God has a plan to save the world of sinners from their sin and its consequences.

4. He came Himself to implement this divine agenda. He wanted us to understand how it works, so He borrowed a body and came the hard way to explain it to us.
5. He's not in a Jewish body anymore; He's in a body called the church, which is made up of individuals who are making sure that every tribe and tongue and nation hears the gospel before the end comes.
6. The end is in sight!

"What's the end?" interrupted the young man. Do you believe that this terrible thing in New York has something to do with the end of the world?"

"I have no idea." I answered. "But I do know that the apostle Paul said in 1 Corinthians 7, 'This world in its present form is passing away' [v. 31]. In another translation it says, 'This world as you see it is on its way out' [*Message*]."

I continued. "Paul paints a very wonderful picture here. The idea is that the world has its sails furled, wrapped tightly around the mast. The world was once driven with the winds of time—its sails full—but now they are furled around the mast, and the world as it is is just going along on its own momentum. It's getting slower and slower, and soon it will stop."

"Well, how soon will it stop?" the young man asked me, somewhat cynically.

"We don't know," I replied. "It's a secret. Even Jesus told us when He was on the earth that only the Father knew. The Bible just says, 'The time is short' (1 Corinthians 7:29). It could be *short* short or *long* short. It could be *middle* short. We just don't know. But one thing we *do* know is that the time is shorter now than when Paul was talking about it. It's shorter than when James said, 'The Judge is standing at the door!' (James 5:9). And Jesus made it sound as if He's got His hand on the doorknob. 'I stand at the door and knock' [Revelation 3:20]."

The young man didn't dismiss this information I was sharing with him, and his cynicism had disappeared when we continued the conversation the next day.

Paul was talking to Christians, not non-Christians, when he wrote to the Corinthians. "The time is short!" The days are evil. Paul didn't expect Christians to dismiss his warning with cynical unbelief, even if nonbelievers did just that. He wanted them to speak Christ into their pagan culture with a new sense of urgency. "Seeing that we don't know how much time we have," the apostle says, "we need to make the most of it for God and His cause. And along the way, as the end approaches, we are warned in Scripture that there *will be* tough times ahead."

Job's story in the Bible is well known, and most people who know it know that he had one of the rawest of deals in life. When deep and terrible trouble came to him and his family "all in a day," his wife told him he should just "Curse God and die" (Job 2:9). We have the same choice when trouble hits. We can either curse God for it and die—or trust God in it and grow!

When trouble hits, we can either curse God for it and die—or trust God in it and grow!

We are responsible to respond to the mysteries of life and death with faith and fortitude, trust and worship. As Job reminds us, it is the Lord who gives, and the Lord who takes away (Job 1:21). What do any of us have that is not received from God anyway? That includes the gift of life itself. When Job's 9/11 came, he fell to the ground in worship. "In all this, Job did not sin by charging God with wrongdoing" (v. 22).

THE FUTURE FACTOR

Along with the tough times come the opportunities that the tough times afford. Paul tells us that the important thing to remember is that the remaining time is very short and so are opportunities for doing the Lord's work (1 Corinthians 7:29). Paul says in essence: "Happiness, sadness, or wealth should not keep anyone from doing God's work" (v. 30). Life is fleeting, as times of trouble remind us. He has numbered our days, and He isn't letting on what number we are up to. This presents an unprecedented opportunity. You can either see an opportunity in every difficulty or a difficulty in every opportunity. If you are tuned in to His agenda, you will be attending to business—His business—day by day as you have the opportunity.

While standing in line in an airport not too long ago, I heard the lady in front of me sharing with her husband some news she had heard on the radio on her way to the airport. It was all bad. Her husband listened and then said, "I don't know what the world's coming to!" I tapped him on the shoulder.

"I do," I said brightly and forthwith told him! The couple listened, astonished, and then Stuart and I engaged them in conversation during the long wait in line.

It's not hard to engage people in conversation. This new normal keeps us ever so slightly on the edge of our seat. We will be in contact with taxi drivers and bellhops, fellow travelers, gas station attendants, waitresses, coaches, and parents at soccer games. We will have tennis partners and exercise buddies, meet parents at PTA meetings, and mix with lawyers and doctors at parties. Friends and relatives will be around at vacation times. It's not that hard!

But of course you won't go to the trouble of possibly offending people or losing friends if you don't believe that Paul was right.

ONLY OLD PEOPLE DIE

One of the things that affected me deeply as I sat on the plane was an inner belief I couldn't shake that only old people die. I had been around long enough to know a few people who had died before their time. The two-year-old down the street who died of leukemia, the teenage anorexic, the eighteen-year-olds in the various wars and military forays around the globe, the victims of traffic accidents I read about in the paper, and, of course, the many lives that have been lost in natural disasters around the world.

Generally we call these deaths untimely. Somehow we believe that a person's life span is indeed three score and ten (a biblical concept from Psalm 90:10) and that any departure before the allotted "due date" is untimely, unfair, and unnecessary.

As I have thought about New York's dark day, I've realized with a jolt that the nearly three thousand people who died in those few short minutes were probably an average age of thirty-five to forty-five years old. So much for my secret belief that only old folk die! (Of course, after working for a relief agency for years, I have realized that this sad world needs campaigns such as "Alive After Five" to raise money for AIDS projects around the world. Millions don't make it past five years of age, never mind thirty-five.)

Perhaps, like me, the Corinthians also believed that only old people die. They weren't so sure about the apostle Paul. He seemed a bit like a fearmonger to them. Why would he be urging young people with their whole of life ahead of them to wait to marry and have a family?

But the church at Corinth had a problem. It was a baby church in all sorts of ways—an immature church in a pagan culture. According to Paul, the Corinthian church talked a lot, knew a lot, gave a lot, worked a lot, and even believed a lot and sacrificed a lot, but they didn't love a lot. And they didn't think a lot—about eternal realities either. They were living very much as they had lived before they became Christians—for the moment.

They were behaving like a bunch of kids. In fact, Paul uses this very comparison. They were behaving like spiritual kids instead of spiritual men. He basically says, "When I was a kid I behaved like one—but then I grew up and became a man." (1 Corinthians 13:11). "Why don't you Corinthians grow up?" he asks. They were bickering, just like kids do. They were saying, "I'm of Paul. I'm of Apollos" (1:12; 3:4). They were people followers rather than God followers. Paul comments, "To be perfectly frank, I'm getting exasperated with your infantile thinking. How long before you grow up and use your head—your *adult* head?" (14:20, *The Message*). "When I became a man, I put childish ways behind me," he says (13:11).

Spiritual gifts do not make spiritual people.

One sign of spiritual immaturity is to be selfish; a sign of maturity is to be selfless. The church in Corinth was spiritually gifted but spiritually immature. Spiritual gifts do not make spiritual people. They were enjoying the gifts of the Spirit to the exclusion of enjoying the Spirit Himself, the Giver of the gifts. It happens today. They were playing with their gifts, and that is understandable—babies play with toys. Paul had his work cut out for him to get them to maturity so that they were others-focused, instead of being self-absorbed. The crisis gave the apostle a chance to challenge them to grow up, to get around to thinking of others rather than themselves and to speak for God into their culture.

Paul had no idea that one day much of this world would be outwardly Christianized. That churches would be attended by too many self-centered people. What he said all those years ago to the Corinthian church has just as much impact now. So Paul, writing to this baby-minded church in a thoroughly anti-Christian culture in a world out of control, says, "If you would wake up, and grow up, and stand up, and speak up, and get up out of your evangelical doldrums, and get on with the job, then this present crisis would prove to be a wonderful opportunity to mature into the image of Christ. This is a spiritual opportunity the likes of which you've never had in your life!"

The same challenge is ours today.

Paul believed that the Corinthians had a choice to

rise to the occasion. He wanted them to look at things positively. He knew that if his new converts would take on his challenge to them, they would see God and themselves and their world in a whole new light. He wanted them to see their own immaturity and be done with it forever. "Be finished with mediocrity and get on with the job," he advised them.

But he also knew that they would get a new perspective only if they let this trouble drive them to God. It's funny how distress can cause us to do three things: see God in a new way, see ourselves in a new light, and see the lost world in a new dimension. The challenge of my particular crisis certainly showed me how intrinsically selfish I am...

Chapter Two

NOTHING CAN HAPPEN TO A CHILD OF GOD OUTSIDE THE WILL OF GOD

The test for me came as the pilot switched on the intercom and announced, "Ladies and gentlemen, all the U.S. airspace is closed. All the borders are closed. We have a national emergency and are making an emergency landing within half an hour."

I looked at my watch and thought, *Where's he going to land? We're over the ocean a few hours out of London!* I remembered my geography and realized we were just over the tip of Newfoundland. Then the strangest thing happened—I immediately began to wonder how many of my fellow passengers knew Christ. How many would go to heaven if we plunged into the ocean? Was this the day?

A verse popped into my head: "All the days ordained for me were written in your book before one of them came to be" (Psalm 139:16). I grabbed my diary and wrote, "Even this day, Lord? Even the eleventh?"

Even this day, Jill. Even the eleventh, He whispered to my soul. As I buckled my seat belt, I felt like I was buckling myself into the will of God, as it were, and a great sense of anticipation and exhilaration began to fill me. The Bible says "all the days" has been ordained for me. Good days, bad days, all days, some days. This day and the next day—*every* day! I revisited my beliefs. Did I believe that nothing could happen to a child of God outside the will of God? Yes, I did. You can't fall out of the will of God. I believed He saw me on that airplane and was ready for any and all emergencies I might experience.

There was nowhere in the world I wanted be at that moment other than in that airplane seat, waiting to see what God had in mind. I began to view God with a new awe. With a whole new understanding. In other words, I got my theology firmly in place. Sometimes our theology is a bit like that Bible that has sat on our shelf forever. We need to blow the dust off it!

Do we really believe what we believe? What did I believe? I wrote in my diary, "Do I believe that God is in control, even when I'm not?" *Yes!* "Do I believe that nothing can happen to His children apart from His permissive will?" *Yes!* "Do I believe that God is good all the time, even when things are bad?" *Yes!* "Do I and other Jesus lovers and glory givers on this plane have a colossal advantage over those who have no High Tower for their soul to run to, no Good Shepherd to calm their beating hearts, no one to hush their fears and remind them that if the very worst were to happen, the very best was yet to come?" Yes, YES, *YES!*

A POOR VIEW OF HEAVEN

As I sat on the plane, uncertain of our landing and our future, I asked myself, "Do I have a poor view of heaven?" Looking back, I think I did. I didn't want to go to heaven just yet! I felt bad thinking those thoughts, and I hoped God wouldn't notice them. We talk loudly about the joy of being with the Lord, but faced with the immediate possibility, we often find ourselves wanting to cling to life—however hardly it may have treated us!

I allowed myself to think of the promises of God and the little I had learned about heaven. And it was a little.

I had written a Bible study for women about heaven, but in my anxiety, I couldn't even remember where the verses about heaven were! But I had enough memories to calm myself and help me to lean on Him in the moment.

One thing I knew: Heaven is the home of the Father, and He had Jesus prepare me a room in His home. Jesus told the disciples as much just before He went back there Himself. Didn't He make that promise to twelve men who were confused and frightened, having just been told by Jesus that He was leaving them? "In My Father's house are many mansions; if it were not so, I would have told you. I go to prepare a place for you…that where I am, there you may be also" (John 14:2–3, NKJV).

As I sat there, I tried to remember a poem I had written about heaven when my mother passed away—I'd even put it in one of my books. Did I believe it? After all, I expected everyone else who bought my book to believe it! I grabbed a pen and scribbled the words on an airplane napkin.

What place is this where rivers flow
And flowers bud and grasses grow?
Where birds compete to praise God's Son,
Where prayers are answered every one.

What place is this where minds at rest
From earth's oppressive battles rest?
Where constant joy is all I know
Where God is everywhere I go?
Where I am overwhelmed to see
The face of Him who died for me!

What place is this where tears are dried?
By hands of Jesus crucified
Where broken dreams are dreamt anew
And come to pass for me, for you?
What place, what place, but home to Him
Who'll make me what I might have been

Then I like Christ at last will grace,
The One I worship on my face.
What place is this? It is His throne
I trust you Lord to bring me home!

Jill Briscoe, *God's Front Door*, Monarch Books

Now, Jill, I lectured myself, *trust Him to open the front door for you when it's time—even if it's today. Trust Him to bring you home.* Peace came quietly then, silently settling into my flurried heart and holding it very still.

The peace He promised. "Peace I leave with you; my peace I give you," He said (John 14:27).

Thank You, Lord, my "held heart" answered.

A right theology of suffering brings comfort. Your theology deals with the fear factor, the frustration factor, and the future factor because of the Father factor. And the Father factor factors in *all* the factors you need to be God's man or God's woman in this present distress, whatever and whenever it might be. You can begin to see God and yourself in a new way, and you begin to see others around you with new eyes, too.

What did I see as I looked around the seats closest to me in the airplane? Some people were as still as statues. A mother and a little girl were holding hands tightly. A businessman on my right was reading a paper—though I suspect he was having a hard time concentrating. And my companion, a young doctor, was thoughtful and quiet.

Knowing that he was a heart doctor, I said, "I hope I'm not going to need you."

He replied with a grin. "I hope I'm not going to need me, either!"

And then we fell silent, wondering what had happened in a world that suddenly seemed forbidding, dark, and unfriendly.

"What do you think this is all about?" he asked me.

"I have no idea."

"What could have closed all the airspace and all the borders?" he mused. "Maybe a nuclear meltdown?"

"Well," I said, "I'm just coming back from Russia, and there were all sorts of reports from missionaries working in Tajikistan that there are camps there with some people called the Taliban making trouble. I believe they are some sort of terrorists."

"But," I added, "how could that have anything to do with this?"

The young doctor nodded. It seemed to have nothing to do with our present dilemma, and we continued guessing and wondering as the pilot made his emergency landing. Imagine our amazement to learn that it did indeed have something to do with the Taliban. The fact that we'd had that conversation opened up opportunities in the week ahead to continue to talk about it together.

During this crisis, I learned that most people rise to the occasion when trouble hits. Strangers become friends (though others respond selfishly and are not much help at all). I learned something about God, about others, and of course about myself. I have to tell you that even though I wasn't disappointed with my response to much of the situation, in some regards I was very ashamed of myself.

For instance, as we landed, the pilot said, "Now, we have to stay on this aircraft until we can be processed. And I'm afraid we've already eaten the two meals provided. We don't have breakfast for you, but we have an emergency ration bar for everyone. We are also okay for water."

The looks on people's faces around the cabin revealed everyone's concern about our situation. Then he said, "We're going to wait to give you the emergency rations because we've no idea if we'll be sitting on the ground five hours or twenty-five hours."

We listened in silence. We were all pretty hungry, as we were overdue for breakfast.

Now, I had some cookies in my purse. And I found myself thinking, *I'll wait until everyone's asleep, and then I'll nibble them a little.* I was horrified at my own sneakiness and began giving myself a stern lecture. *Jill, here you are a Christian writer, author, and speaker! Think of those wonderful God-thoughts you've just enjoyed: "All the days ordained for me is written in your book before one of them came to be." All this "buckling yourself into the will of God" stuff, and now you're busy thinking of nibbling your biscuits surreptitiously while everyone's asleep?*

The flesh rises to the surface at such times, let me tell you! And at that moment, I needed God's Word to the Corinthians through Paul: "Grow up. Just grow up!"

Have you ever heard God say something like that to you? You're hit with some test, and there you are, struggling to react as you should—and failing. And deep in your heart you hear His voice: "Stop being so childish! Grow up. Just grow up!" I would like to think I did grow up a little by the time that particular situation worked itself out.

Overall, my 9/11 experience proved to be one of the most challenging, self-revealing, exciting, productive, stretching, God-shadowed weeks of my life. I trust that because of it, I am better equipped for the next crisis, which is, no doubt, just around the corner of tomorrow.

I WANT TO BE BIGGER

Years ago, Stuart and I were at a friend's house for an evening meal. There were happy chattering kids round the family table telling me about their plans for college and career. The smallest of these, because he was the smallest, was having trouble getting a word in edgewise. Seeing this, his father kindly said to him, "Duncan, you haven't been talking to Mrs. Briscoe. Tell her what *you* want to be when you grow up."

The child looked suitably overcome as all eyes fastened on him. After moments of serious thought, he said, "Bigger!"

We all laughed—we understood Duncan's wish. If only he were bigger, he could get a word in edgewise!

There is no question about it, I grew bigger in Newfoundland. Certainly I was able to settle into the will of God and act on the truth that nothing can happen to a child of God outside the will of God. This helped me relax into the situation, smile at everyone, and invite conversation.

"Home is the will of God for the child of God."

"What have *you* got to smile about?" inquired a lovely young woman who slept on the pew next to me. "I want to go home!"

"I am home," I said.

"What does that mean?"

"Home is the will of God for the child of God," I answered. "Nothing can happen to me without God permitting it. So I'm at home inside wherever I am and whatever happens."

"Tell me about that," she said cautiously.

It was my joy to do so!

Do we want to be bigger? Do we want to leave behind our spiritual immaturity and grow up and join the real world? Do we want to react appropriately to the 9/11s in our lives? To take advantage of the opportunities that abound at such times, to speak Christ into our culture? And how do we keep a sense of urgency to share our faith with other people when the immediate danger is over? After all, how much time did it take all of us to get back to our old normal living once the shock of 9/11 had faded away?

Think about all the people who went to church to pray the week following the tragedy. Churches in America and in many other parts of the world were full of people, believers, skeptics, and everything else in between, who were shocked out of their complacency. They came to pray. It was amazing. But how long did it last? Three weeks? Four? We soon regained our equilibrium and stayed home on Sunday mornings—believers as well as unbelievers!

I think that because of the deteriorating conditions all over the world, we will be kept on "orange alert" in our spirits, and God will work in and through the new normals that will surely come our way as we face up to new paradigms in our lives. I would like to think that Paul's counsel to the Corinthians could now sound a spiritual alarm across the ages and into the hearts of the complacent Christians today. Listen to his words.

Live Single-Mindedly

> The Lord in his kindness has given me wisdom
> that can be trusted, and I will share it with you.
>
> 1 CORINTHIANS 7:25, NLT

The Corinthians' future being dangerous and uncertain, Paul wanted them to think twice before they went ahead developing the relationships they were in. Marriage, after all, doubles your troubles even in the best of times! Paul suggested three things, the first of which was to *live single-mindedly*. "Now those who are married, live as those who are not," he says.

"Those who are married, live as those who are not"? What sort of advice is that? Do I ignore or neglect my spouse? Of course not! In another place, Paul tells us that if a man doesn't provide for his family he is "worse than an infidel" (1 Timothy 5:8, KJV). What he's saying here is that each partner must become single-mindedly God-minded. That means He comes before even your spouse. Jesus put it well: "When your eye is clear, your whole body also is full of light" (Luke 11:34, NASB). In other words, spiritually refocus, even if you're married. Seek enlightenment on how a believing family can speak into the new situation that has developed. If you are a husband or wife, begin to get back to basics where your relationship with God is concerned, and live single-mindedly for Him.

The ethos of my family was always "As for me and my household, we will serve the LORD" (Joshua 24:15). We determined that service would be the thing our family was known for. It wouldn't be Dad serving and Mom watching, or Mom serving while the kids watched. It would be all of us serving together. In other words, our family would be others-oriented rather than us-oriented. We tried to keep in touch with our world and invest our lives in it. We had troubled kids living with us, and there were always enough of them to keep us busy.

Stuart's and my children were witness to a girl who had a baby out of wedlock and boys who were struggling with drug problems. They saw enough of these situations up close to convince them it was not a good idea to abuse alcohol or get girls pregnant or get pregnant themselves.

Our family opened its arms to a needy world of young people, and our kids watched their parents live out their faith putting other people's families before their own. So it was no surprise to watch all three of our kids follow us into ministry. Above all, we had a sense of urgency that the children caught from early days that translated into their own lives: "Serve the Lord while it is day!"

Some other translations render this Scripture this way: "My friends, what I mean is that the Lord will soon come, and it won't matter if you are married or not" (CEV).

Paul wants everyone who is considering the possibility of marriage to look carefully at the partnership they are thinking of forming. Will the woman or man they are choosing in the present be the right partner for the future, however long that future is? Does he or she love Jesus? Do they share the same aspirations and dreams? Paul suggests those who are single rethink the choices they are making in the area of relationships.

He exhorts them not to go ahead with their marriage plans in the present dilemma, with the words "I would spare you." What would he spare them? Well, he wanted to spare them watching their wives and children ripped apart by lions in the arena in Rome, for one thing!

God had the same sort of message to Jeremiah in the Old Testament. "Don't get married," He tells the young prophet (Jeremiah 16:1–2). He tells Jeremiah this because he is living in dark and terrible days. Nebuchadnezzar is about to sack Jerusalem and do terrible things to the women and the children of the city. This sort of trauma is what Paul is trying to spare the Corinthians. So he tells the married as well as the singles to "live single-mindedly."

Simplify Your Life
Secondly, Paul tells the Corinthians to simplify their lives. He suggests that "those who buy something" handle it as though "it were not theirs to keep" (v. 30). Do we usually buy something as though it isn't ours to keep? I don't think so. I know *I* don't. Paul goes even further: "Those who use the things of the world, as if not engrossed in them," or obsessed by them (v. 31).

We live in an obsessed society. We are obsessed with getting, keeping, using…and getting more, keeping more, using more, etc. It's so easy to buy something and become so engrossed with it to the exclusion of all else— until it absorbs all our hours and days. What is it that totally occupies us?

It might not even be an obsession with things. It might be a sexual obsession in which you just can't get enough. And even if you attempt to satisfy the obsession, it leaves you hungrier than ever. You are convinced that the right man or woman, friend or lover, will bring heaven on earth into your life and change everything. But the man or woman you have now can't possibly be the right one because you are still hungry. There is, you see, a God-shaped hole inside you that only a God-shaped God can fill. All the pursuing of obsessions will always leave it empty!

There is, you see, a God-shaped hole inside you that only a God-shaped God can fill.

It may be that you are occupied with your relationships to such an extent that you can't concentrate on anything else. Your anxiety level may be such that there is no energy left for job, service, worship, or even play. Or it may be a simple obsession to avoid pain and embrace pleasure until the vacuum inside you feels filled. All of this clutter in your life, material and nonmaterial, distracts you from the purpose of life itself: to know God and enjoy Him, to know God and love Him, to know

God and serve Him. In other words, we are not to allow this present "crisis"—commerce, pleasure, pain, anxiety over your wife or husband or lack thereof—distract us from the unprecedented opportunity to "seize the day" for Him.

Paul doesn't address the married only about themselves; he talks to the married about the single people. He says, in essence, "Be single-minded like the singles are (or should be), because generally speaking, single people are in a much better position to more easily simplify their life style and live their lives for God." It might not be an advantage a single person wants to embrace, but Paul—single himself—points out the advantages and advises that those who are married follow his example. "Simplify your life; unclutter it," he exhorts. And it's good advice. We all need to deaccumulate.

When we immigrated to the States in 1970, the church that had called us asked us to sell everything and come with little else besides our clothes. They would provide us with a home this side of the Atlantic, which they did. And now we have a house full of clutter *this* side of the pond! It's amazing the propensity we have to clutter up our lives.

When we began packing, I got two suitcases for each

of us and told the kids that one was for their clothes and one was for their precious things.

"But Mommy," Judy said, "I can't get all my dolls in one suitcase!"

It was hard for the kids to pick and choose, and to my chagrin I found that it was hard for their mother as well! I hadn't really noticed all the things I had accumulated—all the wedding gifts and paraphernalia that had collected over thirteen years of marriage. Then there were three kids and a dog and all the things I had acquired along the way, some precious, some not, that all had to be sifted through. I discovered it to be a necessary exercise for me—a useful reminder that without realizing it, I had become cluttered with stuff that was engrossing me. It was time to deaccumulate! In the end, if we aren't careful, things can have us instead of us having things.

Of course, immigrating was quite a motivator. Uncluttering our lives on an ongoing basis is much harder. It takes a determination far greater than mine all those years ago. When you move house—or country—you have no option but to make choices to clear out the attic. But what if you don't move? Then it must be done anyway.

I was in a women's meeting not long ago and asked one of the women, "What are we doing on Saturday night? I see there's no meeting."

"Oh, we're having a clutter auction," she replied.

"What's that?"

The lady explained. "Everybody comes to this retreat with an extra suitcase of clutter, and we have a clutter auction and give the money to missions."

Then and there I determined to return home and begin!

We can unclutter our homes of junk, but we must also work to unclutter our time. That's what Paul means when he says, "Don't be engrossed by the things of this world" (v. 31). Those who buy have no time to enjoy their possessions. Those who buy something must handle it as if they did not possess it (v. 30).

Hold it lightly, folks! Hold it lightly, not tightly.

We clutch and grab, holding on to all our stuff, fiercely protecting all our accumulated things, guarding our precious time, forgetting that time itself is a gift from God. Refusing the art of living simply in a complicated world is to do ourselves and God a disservice. We will never know a fulfilled life. Unfortunately, we often need a crisis in order to make necessary changes.

"But how simple is simple enough?" you ask. That's a good question.

I guess the answer is this: a little bit simpler than last year. You may want to think about downgrading your car, reviewing your vacation plans, investing in a mission enterprise, selling stock for an AIDS relief project. You could take all the clothes you haven't worn for a year and give them to the Salvation Army or cancel your membership in the health club and walk in the park instead. You could put your TV in storage for a year. (One of my friends did this and spent the time taking a Bible correspondence course instead.)

You could quit buying any more stuff for your kids for birthdays or Christmas and give them some of their inheritance ahead of time. Enjoy it with them—furniture, jewelry, or keepsakes they would otherwise have only when you are six feet under!

Or you could give them *time* with you instead of things from you.

If our lives are cluttered up with not only material things and concerns but also relationships or schedules—plans that exclude God—we need to take our calendar off the wall and reprioritize. We need to get on our knees and ask God what to remove from our schedule. Then when the empty spaces appear, ask the Lord how to fill them. Sometimes the answer will be to fill them with Him!

So in order to live single-mindedly, unclutter your life. Whatever it takes, simplify your life. And then you will have made time and space available to revel in God.

Revel in God

Because distresses in our lives make us aware of eternal issues over material ones, we have a wonderful opportunity (whether we are single or married) to simplify our lives and revel in God. "Attend upon the Lord without distraction," as Paul puts it (1 Corinthians 7:35)—and this not halfheartedly.

Paul says that married people will find this a lot harder. Married folks have a lot more things to distract them. Single people have it made because they can attend upon the Lord without distraction (1 Corinthians 7:32). It's wonderful to be married. What a gift from God! But sometimes those blessed distractions of ours—husbands, wives, and children—can be a problem as we struggle to live single-mindedly, simplify our lives, and revel in God.

A while ago, we had the whole family with us, seventeen people including children and adults. It was a wonderful three days together. We were going to church on the final day, and our daughter was helping me clean up the place and get the breakfast dishes done.

I looked at my watch. "Hey Judy, we have to get ready for church. We've had these three glorious, marvelous days with the family, but I haven't had time to say one word to you. We've been too busy with the kids. Come and let's get ready together. Let's steal some time for us!"

What she said stopped me in my tracks.

Judy grinned. "Mom, I was hoping you'd ask me."

I realized that we'd been so busy with the family that we hadn't made sure to take time to revel in each other. Judy and I have an incredibly close relationship, yet we hadn't stolen away or snatched a single moment just to shut the door and giggle and laugh together, enjoying each other as a mom and daughter should.

Do you know what reveling in God is? It's God saying to you, "You've been so busy with My "family," but what about *us*? He's hoping you'll ask Him for some "us" time. And He can't wait to say to you, "I was hoping you'd ask Me!"

When was the last time you just reveled in your relationship with God? You might have an incredible relationship with Him but are so busy with His family, His people, that you don't make time for Him. Do you need to address this? The busier we get with the church, the more time we need to attend upon the Lord without distraction (1 Corinthians 7:35).

"Martha, Martha" Syndrome

Jesus had a problem when He was in Bethany. He was getting some time with His disciples to teach them about reveling in Him—to enjoy His company. Both male and female disciples had come together in Martha's house. It was a favorite place to be.

Now, Martha was busy being single—but Martha was also busy being busy! One day when she was hosting Jesus, she found herself a bit like I did when I had the family for the weekend and had no time to breathe. Perhaps she had uninvited guests staying. Perhaps she had known she would need to feed twelve hungry disciples, but she probably didn't bargain for the hangers-on! There would be the lepers Jesus had healed the last time He was in Bethany who would want to thank Him. And there would be the people Jesus hadn't healed and helped yet who wanted to be healed and helped! The relatives of the lepers and all who had been cleansed, like Simon, would bring gifts and would want some of Jesus' time too, and Martha's party list grew and grew.

Jesus was sitting, hoping Martha would leave it all and just give Him ten minutes of her time. He was hoping she would ask Him. But how could she possibly break away when there was all this serving to do? And it was all made worse by Mary opting out of her responsibilities in order to respond to His invitation to sit at His feet (the posture of a disciple) and listen to His word.

She attended to the Lord in the middle of the muddle, and Jesus commended her for it.

This frustrated Martha no end. In a modern translation, she says to the Lord, "Doesn't it bother you that my sister has left me to do all the work by myself?" (Luke 10:40, CEV). I think Martha would have given her right arm to sit at Jesus' feet, but someone had to do the work! The point Jesus made was "Really, Martha? Why? The work will get done, maybe not on time, but it will still be there when the most important things have been attended to."

Mary chose to do the hard thing. She chose to step out of the expectations of her role and the expectations of the disciples and her sister and be concerned only about the expectations of Jesus. She attended to the Lord in the middle of the muddle, and Jesus commended her for it and rebuked Martha for rebuking Mary and not following her example!

"Martha, Martha," He said, "you are worried and upset about many things, but…Mary has chosen what is better, and it will not be taken away from her" (Luke 10:41–42). Luke tells us: "Martha was distracted with much serving" (v. 40, NKJV). Isn't that a familiar dilemma for the Christian? To be distracted from the One we serve by the very serving we offer! It's so easy to do. What we do for Jesus must never take the place of the Jesus we're doing it for. And what we do for Jesus' family must not distract us from the most important thing, either.

First, we must recognize our neglect of "the most important thing" and redress the situation. The secret lies in Jesus' words to Martha concerning Mary. "She *chose* what is better" (Luke 10:42, emphasis added). It's simple. No matter how busy you are, don't be distracted by busyness as you serve the Lord.

Remember, Martha was single, and she too was distracted. So we come back to the "whether you are single or married"—we have a choice on a daily basis. What is it to be? The Lord is waiting for us to wait upon Him. We mustn't keep Him waiting!

Only you can make that choice. Don't let work and service make that choice for you! But what are you supposed to do once you're sitting at His feet?

Just enjoy Him!

Chapter Three

ENJOY GOD FIRSTHAND

How do you revel in God? What does that mean? It means you enjoy God *firsthand*, not secondhand. You hear His footfall with the inner ear of faith and run to meet Him. Reveling in Him means enjoying just being together and giving yourselves time. That takes more than a glance heavenward first thing in the morning before you fly out the door to work!

Walk together early, before the break of day. Sit in a rocker in the silver silence of the dawn light, and break bread together. Admire His sky painting, the work of His fingers. Smell the flowers in the hedgerow. Listen to the robin in the tree. Watch the clouds together. Or just sit still by the fire and enjoy each other's company. Perhaps you will soon find the silence of love quieting you down, for it's only in the silence that you are able to hear His footstep.

But even in the bustle of the doings of the day, you can school your heart to meet Him in the silent places of your heart. Like Mary, if a silent place in the world is impossible to find, go to Him in the noisy place. We, of course, have a huge advantage over Mary and Martha in that Christ abides within, in the deep place where nobody goes, within in our souls—the interior place where we discover Him and hear Him say, "I was hoping you'd come to talk. I was hoping you'd ask Me!"

It's only in the silence that you are able to hear His footstep.

And it's not just for His sake we must do this, but for ours. He is hoping we will ask Him for an eternal moment of His time for *our good.* He knows that we cannot survive our frenetic busyness if we don't stop spinning our wheels and slow our spirits down. Professor Carl Jung once observed, "Hurry is not of the devil; hurry is the devil." Prayer braves the depths of our inner life and invites us to be still and know that He is God (Psalm 46:10). Above all, prayer is a declaration of our dependence on God. It isn't something mechanical you do; it is somewhere you go to meet Someone you know.

First, you put yourself intentionally into His presence. Now, I know that we are always in His presence, but you need to find a quiet corner and realize that fact. The first thing is to be still, and the second is to be quiet. When you do that, He will somehow, someway, tell you, show you, and remind you that He is God.

Find a place if you can. If, like Mary on the day the Lord came to dinner, you can find only one option, then meet Him in your soul in the middle of the muddle. Usually there are options. It should be fairly easy here in America, with our big houses and spaces outside, to plan ahead and schedule a time and place for these "God encounters." If I were talking about other cultures, where it is well-nigh impossible to find a square inch without someone in it, it would be different, but there is absolutely no excuse not to find a quiet place near at hand at least three or four times a week. Once you make the effort to find that place, go there and be quiet.

QUIETUDE IS A LEARNED ART

Quietude is a lot harder to find than a time and a place. But it must be found if we are to practice the art of waiting on God. As a culture, we aren't used to quiet. In fact

I think we are frightened of it. Look at the kids walking down the city streets or even in the countryside. Earphones are seemingly surgically attached to their ears feeding them noise morning, noon, and night. They study to noise, they play to noise, they exercise to noise, and they sleep to noise. And it is mostly loud noise. Whether pleasant or unpleasant noise, it succeeds in focusing the attention on itself to the exclusion of most other things happening around them. And as soon as the headphones are out of the ears, they are replaced by a cell phone.

Quietude is indeed a learned art. It has always been so, but it seems no one is signing up for courses on it, and even fewer are teaching them!

In the quiet, you will hear His voice—the still, small voice of God—and it will be unmistakable. But you'll never hear it unless you turn off the noise. Not just turn it down, but turn it off!

Ask yourself when the last time was you heard the birds sing, the rustle of tall grass, or the buzzing of bees. When was it last that the whispers of the wind in the trees prepared your spirit to hear His Spirit? Most people you ask will probably be hard-pressed to tell you when they last allowed the music of nature to whisper His coming. Yes, these are nature's noises, but they are quieting noises that can somehow prepare you for the quietest noise of all: the sound of the still, small voice of God.

Note that it is the *still,* small voice of God (1 Kings 19:12). It's interesting that the Scripture uses that word *still.* I'm not sure what a still voice sounds like, but I know it when I "hear" it, and it stills me. It is His voice, who is standing still within me waiting for me to be still enough to listen. He waits for me to stop spinning and settle my mind down. It's a voice that isn't rushing around inside me demanding to be heard; it's standing still in my heart, drawing me down into an incredible pool of peace that passes all understanding.

> *I need to be still in order to hear the stillness of God.*

I need to be still in order to hear the stillness of God. I need to be quiet because His voice will not thunder over the noise of the world. And once I am quiet and still—like the very voice of God—I will know that "God is." No one needs to say it in words. I will just *know* it. It's a wonderful knowing, as if you just had a long conversation with the best-loved friend in the world. Yet not a human word has been spoken, just a silence louder than words.

You will know at that moment that God is God and you are not. More than that, you *know* God with a spiritual intimacy that is like a deep conversation without words. It's an incredible experience of just knowing that you are loved beyond measure and that you and God are locked into this fantastic silver space, where neither needs to use words to understand what is being said. Just being still and quiet is enough.

NO WORDS SPOKEN, BUT VOLUMES SAID

Some of the most intimate moments of my marriage have been when Stuart has been on a ministry journey. He comes home and we meet in a busy airport. He walks through the international terminal door, and we get our arms around each other and hold each other so tightly. We just stand there very still and quiet. No words are spoken and yet volumes are being said. Movement spoils the moment; words break the spell. Yes, chaos is going on all around us, but it cannot intrude into the circle of our love and joy at being together again.

On an obviously deeper level, the same happens when we are still and know that He is God. The meeting might be in a busy airport or at the hearth in front of a fire. We just sit and without words speak to each other, look at each other, maybe cry, laugh, and just *know* each other. I believe this is one aspect of worship. The art is then to take that deep awareness, the tangible evidence of the presence of God, from that encounter into the day.

In a marriage, two people cannot physically be in the same place at the same time all day long—there are things to do and places to go—but we savor the memory of being together and eagerly look forward to being there again as soon as possible. The same is true of our time with the Lord. As we go about our daily doings, we can simply lean back into that safe love and bask in the richness of the gift of it, remembering our time together and seeking it out again.

So find a place and make the time, and in the quietness listen to the voice of the living God. You will never be the same. And remember, with these things in place, when whatever will happen *happens*, life will go on.

Chapter Four

LIFE GOES ON

The seventh chapter of 1 Corinthians tells us to continue on (vv. 17, 24) in the situation we find ourselves at this moment of eternal history with a sharpened awareness of the presence of the Lord, a pared-down lifestyle, and a determination to see our part through whatever and whenever the end may be!

Paul is emphasizing that we should continue on with a sharpened focus in our personal relationships with each other. In this present crisis, he says, "Life goes on." If you are in some sort of crisis, waiting for the end to come, don't change your marital status. Be on high alert and ready for anything, reorganize your life, revisit your devotional disciplines. Celebrate God and revel in Him!

The Christmas following September 11, I was given

a little book of photographs of the Second World War. The images triggered all sorts of memories in my mind. As the news came over our TVs in the States that Christmas about the anthrax scare, I was taken back. I remembered my mother's voice as I went out the door to school every morning. "Jill, have you got your homework?"

"Yes, Mum."

"Have you got your lunch?"

"Yes, Mum."

"Have you got your gas mask?"

"Yes, Mum."

That was our new normal back then, and taking our gas masks to school was all part of it.

Life goes on.

And in this new normal, life will go on.

DOING THE NORMAL THINGS

In abnormal times, there is peace of mind to be found in doing the normal things of life. Life goes better if you keep to a familiar routine.

During the war, for example, Mother would pick up the morning paper and decide what we should see of the news of the day. Often she would read it with us. The pictures of the Blitz in London were pretty graphic.

I remember one time seeing a picture of our library in the middle of town. The roof had been blown off the building by a bomb the previous night. "Mum!" I said, aghast. "That's our library. The roof's been blown off!"

About a week later my mother said, "Get your coat on, Jill. It's library day!"

"But Mother, don't you remember? The roof's been blown off the building."

"That's all right. We'll go anyway," she replied cheerfully. "They'll have cleared up the mess by now. Life goes on, Jill, and we are to continue."

We embraced the normal things, and in that abnormal situation, we found a way to cope and move forward.

DON'T QUIT

One of the failings in our society is that it takes so little for us to quit. We don't continue on. Our kids don't finish the food on their plates. We start a course at the YMCA and quit a few weeks in. We sign up for a magazine and then read only the first five issues. We determine (mostly at the start of the year) to attend church more regularly, but after a few weeks we start sleeping in again (it's our only day off, and doesn't the Bible say it's supposed to be a day of rest?).

I remember seeing a poster in a teenager's room. It portrayed a young boy in football gear sitting dejectedly on the bench after a game. It obviously had not been a very good game. Across the top of the poster were the words "I quit." At the base of the poster were the words "I DIDN'T" superimposed over a cross.

He didn't, did He?

When Christ's 9/11 came, He didn't give up or quit.

When Christ's 9/11 came, He didn't give up or quit. And He did it so that *we* wouldn't have to quit when the tough times come and our private world falls apart. Yes, it's tough to put a relationship on hold for no other reason than that it's better for the King and the kingdom in this present time to stay married or to stay single, but in the power of the risen Christ it can be done. This or some other sacrifice can be made. We need to continue on with God and for God and not quit.

THE MILKMAN

Do you remember the milkman? (If you do, you're probably a little older, like me.) Go on, admit it! Remember when the milkman used to deliver milk door-to-door from his milk cart? He had those wire trays that you put the bottles in when they were empty, and he would pick them up after we put them out on the back step and deliver the fresh milk every day.

One day, in wartime Liverpool, the picture in the paper was of a milkman in London. He was delivering the milk. I gazed at the picture. Not a single house in sight was standing. But the milkman was doing his thing and whistling a tune as he scrambled over the rubble, making his way to the burnt-out, smoking remains of the few houses left half standing.

Had his house been hit, we wondered? We didn't know. But he had a job to do, and he was doing it. He was continuing on because life goes on. And we need to do the same. If a crisis comes, we need to continue on as we were before it happened.

Another picture that sticks in my mind was of four men in business suits standing amid smoking ruins. "It's the stock exchange," my mother said matter-of-factly, as if I, at the age of six, would understand what the stock exchange was! But I understood the all-too-familiar picture of the smoking ruins.

"What are the men doing?" I asked her

"They are looking at plans to put the building up

again," she answered quietly. "Life goes on, Jill. Life goes on! When the enemy bombs one of our buildings, we just build it all over again."

Now I am an adult (and an elderly one at that), I have seen how this applies to so many situations in life. When you are in the middle of a crisis and you find yourself standing in life's ruins, turn to the Great Architect and say, "Let's build!"

Christians should respond differently than unbelievers to the devastation caused by the enemy of our souls. Christians should think differently about waking up one morning and finding all we worked for in a smoldering heap of ashes. We should get out the milk cart and begin delivering milk, whistling a tune as we go!

GREAT CLOUD OF WITNESSES

For the past five years my husband, Stuart, and I have been flying all around the world as ministers-at-large for our church. We respond to invitations from all continents and are trying to support and help the church in the developing world. This year we have met God's people from Israel and Jordan, Australia and the Philippines, China and the UK, Russia, Mexico, and Cuba, to name a few. Their stories would fill volumes.

Stories of how Jesus walked into their lives or their dreams and they came to know Him. These stories are easy listening.

But then there are stories of the terrible misuse and abuse of believers for no other reason than to try to make them renounce their faith. These stories are not so easy to listen to. Many times I want to shout, "Stop! It's too terrible to hear!" And yet these men and women tell their stories of torture and courage with a gleam in their eyes and a set to their spiritual chins that defies description. After their ordeals, some have been offered freedom to leave the country, but they refuse. "We must stay," they tell us earnestly. "The people in the church need us."

We have met mere children who have watched their parents butchered but who have been loved well by a church that itself is in constant danger. Churches with tragic stories to tell that almost defy description, but who are singing their pain away and continuing on. "Life goes on," they tell us loudly and clearly. "God is strengthening our backs to bear this suffering." The church worldwide is in good shape, mostly allowing the Spirit to work His work through them in their own difficult culture and time.

And even here in America the next generations of young believers are coming out of the ruins of divorce that have demolished the twin towers of marriage and family. They are rising up and deciding to raise the building up again. They're vowing to stay pure until they are married and never to be ashamed of Jesus in this increasingly angry and hostile world. And they are loving God with all they've got!

The church of our day has its own young heroes and heroines—of Columbine High School, Iraq, the tsunami, and unknown, unsung others whose pictures grace the walls of God's hall of fame in heaven. Historically, the church of Jesus Christ has always done better when the heat is on. We must not fail the "great cloud of witnesses" (Hebrews 11) that have gone before us and are cheering us on from the grandstands of heaven. We *must* continue on, finish the race, and receive the prize of the high calling of Jesus Christ (Philippians 3:13–15).

In this new normal, we are to be on high alert, ready for anything.

HE WILL NOT FALL OVER

In this new normal, we are to be on high alert, ready for anything. For Christians are really engaged in two wars. In the last days, we are told, we "will hear of wars and rumors of wars" (Matthew 24:6). More and more people will not only hear of them; they will find themselves in the middle of them! We are told not to be afraid. That may be easier said than done.

Some of these conflicts will be on earth, while others will take place in the unseen world. We can safely let the wars in the heavenlies be overseen by Him who has everything in heaven and earth in His control through His holy angels. We are to engage in this spiritual warfare with spiritual weapons—the Sword of the Spirit, which is the Word of God, and a faith that moves mountains. We are to pray without ceasing and battle on our knees against an unseen yet very real enemy. These wars outside our control are supervised by Him, and He has promised that the ultimate war will be won.

It is the war within the human heart that we fight on a daily basis. This must be *our* responsibility. We must take charge of our lives and look within ourselves and see what is going on. Panic and fear have no place in the heart of a Jesus lover and glory giver. Remember that God is never surprised. He knows the future as thoroughly as He knows the past and has provided for us. He has everything in hand, and we should lean on Him.

He will not fall over!

I Am Home

I had cause to remember my own words this year. I was standing in the immigration hall in Bangalore, India, waiting eagerly to meet Stuart, who had gone ahead of me and was waiting for me there. I turned to get my papers and passports out of my computer case. The zipper was open, and everything had disappeared. My two passports were gone, my round-the-world airline tickets, my identification, my money—everything.

I ran out of line to the desk and asked the man in the glass booth to stop the people who were going through into the reception area. "I've been robbed," I explained. "It has to be someone in this hall!" They wouldn't listen, and they didn't believe me. Thus began a nightmare of red tape—and the horrible experience of having lost my identity and being suspect to the officials. They didn't believe that I had been robbed, that I was Jill Briscoe, or that I had a husband patiently waiting outside the airport who could vouch for me. In fact, they didn't see any reason I had a right to enter India at all. They took me by the arms, turned me around, and tried to put me back on the plane to deport me to Frankfurt! It was my own mini 9/11! *Very* mini, it is true, but nevertheless a crisis of sorts.

It's a horrid thing not to be believed. To be treated with considerable suspicion and rudeness. It took three weeks to sort it all out. I eventually entered the country, but without an entry visa. I did nothing I had gone to India to do and spent interesting and frustrating times in police stations, consulates, and Indian taxis and hotels trying to get a passport and exit visa to get out of a country I was now sorry I had gotten into in the first place!

Eventually, sitting at the Bombay airport an hour before my hoped-for plane took off for home, having missed all the planned engagements all over the country, and having not a clue *why* all this apparent waste of time, energy, and recourses had been allowed, I wondered if I would ever get out of India. My husband had left to ful-fill our engagements without me, and I wondered mournfully if he would come and visit me once a year for the rest of my life if the authorities decided not to let me leave! A man appeared and said, "Where is the stamp that tells me you entered India?"

For the umpteenth time, I explained that no one would give me an entry or exit stamp because I had been robbed in the immigration hall before entering the country and so on. He looked at me and said, "You are not here then! And if you are not here, you cannot leave the country." At that he smiled and walked away.

Well, I thought, *if that's true—and I'm truly not here—no one will notice if I get on the plane with the rest of the passengers who are boarding!*

I walked up to the agent with my heart in my mouth and gave her my ticket and temporary passport. She opened it looking for the exit visa, which wasn't there. Next she looked for the entry visa, which wasn't there either, and shook her head. A friend had helped me get some sort of stamp, and she was looking at it in a puzzled fashion.

Lord, if You want me here longer, okay, I managed to pray (with not too much enthusiasm). *I do believe that nothing can happen to a child of God outside the will of God,* I added, remembering September 11. *Therefore this airport gate is exactly where I need to be! I am home.*

I found myself internally relaxing into the will of God for me.

The girl looked around for her supervisor but couldn't find her. She looked back at me. I smiled a great big smile. She smiled back and then waved me through onto the airplane. I whistled a little tune like the milkman and continued on. Settling myself gratefully into my seat, I went to the deep place inside me where nobody goes. My favorite place.

He was waiting for me. And there I thanked God and reveled in Him!

1-59052-234-6

RUNNING ON EMPTY?

You know what it's like to feel drained. Out of steam. Out of options
and ideas. God has given us what we need to fill up when we run low.
It's the incredible gift of Himself. In this engaging book, Jill Briscoe
guides you to a source of ample sustenance.

Even as you empty yourself, the Holy Spirit will fill you. And in giving
yourself away, you will find life.

www.bigchangemoments.com

STUART BRISCOE

No one has time to do it all. Discover how
to effectively evaluate your priorities so that the
concerns of this world will never again steal
your valuable time!

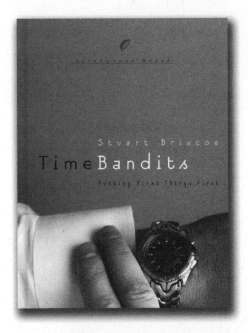

TIME BANDITS
Putting First Things First
ISBN: 1-59052-403-9